Beasts of the Hill

Beasts of the Hill

Mark Neely

Oberlin College Press
Oberlin, Ohio

The FIELD Poetry Series, vol. 28
Oberlin College Press, 50 N. Professor Street, Oberlin, OH 44074
www.oberlin.edu/ocpress

Cover and book design: Steve Farkas.
Cover art: Pete Christman, "Lola."

Library of Congress Cataloging-in-Publication Data

Neely, Mark, 1971-
Beasts of the hill / Mark Neely.
    p. cm. -- (The Field poetry series; vol. 28)
Includes bibliographical references.
ISBN-13: 978-0-932440-44-0 (pbk. : alk. paper)
ISBN-10: 0-932440-44-4 (pbk. : alk. paper)
I. Title.
PS3614.E36B43 2012
811'.6--dc23
                        2011048678

for my parents

Contents

Beasts of the Hill

Four Falls

The royal sky (only maples with their orange brushes bring) reminds me of a pair of eyes, the bare dogwood of teasing stray hairs back in the dark. I used to talk all night. Shouldn't I know more now, have more to say? For twenty years I didn't write down one thing. If this is summer dying, then the forecast must be sad and beautiful, or bloody, loud, painful—like a giant being born.

Garage roof, bike ramp, the high rickety fence of the three-legged dog. Once I wrapped my face in cotton and did a stuntman down the stairs. The day my mother's friend went missing. They found her maroon bike in a ditch. They thought I was psychic when I saw a mouse sniffing corn leaves in her hair. She always dies. The farmer always finds her body. I see him kneeling there.

Mist speckles my face like lice from the giant's hair. The tour book says I should feel both exhilarated and insignificant, but the sausage gravy from my hotel breakfast isn't sitting right. My eyelids itch from last night's champagne. I'd rather be back at the hotel, watching *SportsCenter* in my overstuffed bed, so unless some asshole goes over in a barrel, I'm not going to feel a fucking thing.

Late at night the screen goes purple as a desert flower and I'm diving again, sliding down the wormhole into what dimension? From the silvery bottom I peer up at a square of sky, hear the backhoe backing up to fill me in. Kids who dive into wells must dream wet walls forever. Like a bat swooping from its attic, I'm half falling, half in flight. What Friday nights are for, my calling.

Funeral

We file around the coffin
like a buffet line. A bad
buffet, everything
picked over. Until the

daughter's breathing
fills the basilica
and the whole space
lifts off, a ship

on a huge swell.
In a storm of music
we lash the hysteric
daughter to the mast.

Self-Portrait with Straw Hat

When I cut my throat—a fiddler
bowing short his final note—

I'll do it in July under that black
maple where we used to marvel

and my blood will seep down
to the spear-tipped roots to be

carried skyward with whatever
other mist my body holds.

In February, Bernard will tap the tree,
boil the sap into syrup.

I have given him your address
so he can send a bottle.

Four Fields

Those locust trees could hiss like snakes, then still to painted leaves—the wind playing with its paper toys. A skinny pine in an ivy-sequined gown took me by the hand and led me down where rows of corn abided between wood and road, to show how easily a life can spring from soil. I was more fox than human then, stalking the treeline for black-berries, grasshoppers and squirrels.

Of course the sun was brilliant! All summer it taught the beans their sup-plicant green dance, it beat the dirty page of road where Grandfather's rust bucket broke the light. He rat-tled by and lifted one Midwestern finger from the wheel to say hello. I stood in dust, each mote a silver stone, watching the loose bumper bounce above the road. The old man going to hitch up to the fire.

Most summer nights I sat on the barn roof at dusk as the dog ran rodents into burrows or worried birds up trees, and a white moon drilled a hole in the receding day. Now I try to say the name of everything—redbud, brushfoot, northern flicker, cockspur, prairie vole. Back then I couldn't care less about all that, pleased enough with moon and sun, rat and cardinal, jackrabbit and crow.

Here and now the silence has a human shape. Beetles undermine the house in threes and threes. A dark shape flaps in a black shrub then silences its fear. Another godless sky descends. I know a hidden animal makes the clearest sounds. The hoot owl asks *how,* not *who.* A black train screams by, its hulking ghost, but these birds won't scare. They sit like tumors on the branches.

Lovers' Meal

The head
rolled across the dirt
like a cap popped off a beer.

Its blood flowed
down the crevices of
our chopping stump.

*That is how canyons
are made,* I thought,
as you held

the flapping
body away from
your yellow dress.

Einstein's Alphabet

Afternoon breeds
curtains; deviant evening
forages grain here

in January's
kaleidoscopic last
move. Night opens,

pulling quarry.
Rise stars!
Teach us

void's worn
xerography.

Your zealot.

Four Blues

The trouble is I bore Picassos silly. At a painter's party the guests all look painted themselves—their faces great roaring abstract oceans, or delicate nudes with lines like bleached police chalk, all shadow and suggestion. I huddle in a corner, so obviously written, clutching the bird-leg of my martini. *Honey,* says my vicious friend Virginia, *no one has time to curl up for days and read you.*

The song goes on even in my sleep like a trumpet player in a basement bar who sits over a bowl of rags, skin buzzing from the drug, while the bartender settles the register over a long whiskey. The player's woman gone. Run off with a goddamn plumber. She used to wake up when he came to bed. The trumpet licks he made of her, humming as the white shades glowed and shook above the bed.

Months of January bring the walking blues. To start and start like my daughter trying out the alphabet. She's all beginnings now. If I'm lucky I have a speck of middle left. Time to visit Morelia, go back to Maine where honeymooners meditate on frozen stones, walk Rajgir for Buddha's lesson, or Oriole Street where kids sing baseballs through air. Time for Cairo. Sad, exotic Kankakee.

When I stand on the morning's scale it says how old I am and what a punk, as the lights blink *ordinary, ordinary, only worse.* The violets on the bathroom wallpaper pucker. I'll tear them out this summer or the next. Without measure I would lift off like a heron over water. I sulk here glowering at my iron wings. But after a night of gin and reckoning, I often trip a few notes up the clouds.

I Pick a Fist-Fight with the Sky

Fucking mist, fucking falling
leaves, this maw of morning swallowing

me whole. These trees aren't on
my side—*Shut up,* they say, *and listen.*

Fucking acorns cracking off the roof.
Deer hunker in their thickets.

My love twirls
noodles in swank restaurants

or wakes up late
and musses her hair

for some tall man
grinning at the sun.

But this song's a spiritual, okay?
Oh house of grace, kingdom of a thousand

secret entrances, I'm going
to kick your front door's teeth in,

thrash the many-eyed guards
and bluster through each florid

room until I find my dead
and drag them out . . . but here

go the goddamn trees
again, the snickering rain,

here comes the storm
to knock my lights out.

Four Mirrors

I woke up this morning, feeling so sick and bad,
Thinking about the good times I must have had.
—Son House

Damn traffic jam when I'm already late for work. On Locust Street, home of dentists and deans, where typically a few sedans breeze past cheery dog-walkers. Today it looks like a stalled state funeral. In front of a fallen-in Victorian, a ruffled boy chases an actual peacock in and out of the road. The boy moves like a crazed cat. The peacock, in his madness, is not half as beautiful as you might imagine.

Nothing yet on the sinking ferry; nothing on the indecent Act; nothing on the starved teen idol; nothing on the cancer in our soda, in our cell phones, in our air; nothing on the amputees of war; nothing on the alley mentalists who terrify my sleep; nothing yet on sand-veiled cannons; nothing on the peeps under my floors; nothing at all from Tokyo; nothing from the game but this: no score.

On Food TV the counters are wide and bright with vegetables— little marbles, marvels, in colored ramekins. *Dishes from Asia demand preparation*, says the chef through perfect lips. She leans over the oil to hear it whisper *broccoli, garlic*. We dash home, open cans and slap something together, as noted by all the other networks. But at the first taste of gin, I still pause and thank the ancestors.

My coffee is no crystal lake, thank God, where I can see my face. I take it muddy, with huge spoonfuls of amnesia. At night I stumble through dream wrecks, wrenching glass and metal from beloved bodies. Men grow crueler every year. New ways to kill and rape are television novelties, brilliant birds. Through these greasy windows the trees look half past dead. Still I want to live one more day.

Cardinal

May not be rare but I'm the bird of Illinois,
Indiana, five other states to boot. I shake

my mottle, stink, flutter, and squeak
an off-key song—a grave noise

like your oldest smoker saying *wheat.*
You have to have the nose for it, or ear,

the eyes for it, one for each flap of your hat.
It's under there you keep requirements

for houses, for the dolls your daughters plead
for on your holiday—you paint it

red, right? Huff around in green sweaters.
That's how you celebrate your noble dead?

I flash lung blood against the sky instead,
or kindle in the brush, your furious desire.

Family Story

It's hell in the city of gold . . .
—Agha Shahid Ali

To the brother's
house in Amherst
each one goes

to die. Or guts
of airplanes
fly their corpses

home. Above the
jumbled cargo,
passengers nod

into magazines,
holding like teacups
their little whiskey bottles.

Four Years

That one slick as the body of a jet, shredding the sky's thick music. An easy winter. In spring we spent late nights soaking up the smog, its connoisseurs, then endured the Chicago heat-wave in our sweltering third-floor. On the South Side Polish grandmothers died, too scared to crack their windows. Our favorite bar lost power for a week. We drank at home in boiling candlelight.

The next we could not bear to speak. We took it casually, tried to board the plane, but its skin was gone, it was all ribs and light. I thought career. I thought therapy. I thought foreign country, finished, facelessness. We settled in a fog of Scandinavian descent, where gaunt dogs nipped the fences as we passed. You threw dice in alleys with leering men. I covered my mouth with a claw.

Light beams filled with dust without you. Cockroaches crawled around slow as babies in the heat. I turned my sign to *Closed,* but you showed up anyway in heels and shiny dresses. I pulled hair from corn, lit the same end of a cigarette a thousand times. The ice storm killed our elm. Thank God for the ghost-scent of lilacs, my skin for staying on, the rusty sink for keeping my hands clean.

A killing, you said, after we banned all verbs. One in a million times that works. You searched the attic for your grandmother's diary. A few months later, you floated from the grocery store before I could jump behind a tree. You said *you*, I said *me*. The next generation can work it out. Then you hopped on your blue bicycle and disappeared around a bend. I thought that only happened in a song.

Inside a Pine

Sun through a thousand
needles loosens
the sap, washes out
jeans and lightens

tiny arm hairs
where insects
hide, ride us
to our graves.

Where I hide,
my mother's muffled
voice falling from
the kitchen window

breaks through the static
of my rickety escape pod.
All the birds go off
like bleeping gauges.

Poem Scratched in an Old Foundation

We reached a city where all signs
were blown down
Notices once staple-gunned to phone poles
blew around our heads like blasted
feathers so now and then a word
a brand name
brushed my face

Looters had been through all the buildings
All the windows gone
They even took the useless
screwplates from the sockets

Under a ruined billboard's scrawny legs
I found a rock bowl filled with water
You were laughing as you drank the rain
and I thought of that actress
you looked like when we first met in the library
worlds ago

I looked up at the white impression
the sun made on the fog
and laughed along with you
for nothing could be worse
than where we'd been

Four Shades

Only the worst flu-fevers bring back thoughts of 'ninety-eight but when they come no pounded tuber or ablution can dull the blues that pool around my bed. I pour these oils warily, cover the canvas with eyes. I hear you toured the Alps, fixed up a house, your handy husband. You write glum stories on a Royal. Is that true? And you nuked me in the rumor war. You know what? Fuck you too.

On the mountainside the trees cough up black smoke that settles in depressions like Van Gogh. Black ash coats woodsheds and truck beds and propane tanks and the inside of my nose. There is no Hollywood royalty here, just hippies, loggers, separatists, so the chopper drops a few buckets but the smokejumpers stay in their rooms. We don't believe in firefighters anyway. We believe in rivers.

Paint me green, lean with envy of he who did what I could not—scored, hired on, took the lady's hand. Make a scene. A grievous carapace skulks under heavy leaves, charged college kids splashing by in snazzy cars. My famous friend brings me to a bright hall lined with clever paintings. I should enjoy it—I once adored novels, after all, even some poems. I'm a roach inside a crystal ball.

I'm praying again, laying paltry bribes at the feet of winged border guards. I read the book backward so I remember how it started pretty well, but not the end. In the beginning there were caves where filthy women laid eggs for sooty brainless men. Then we invented hay and horses, ringtones. We invented politician hair. And burning your own house for the insurance. And great books courses.

More News from the Flood

I swam in the fumes,
elbowed through an endless funeral
where a band played from the back
of a bombed-out bus, danced

through the corpse-field
with a woman in a dirty dress,
so drunk I thought the sun
a tennis ball I had thrown into the sky

in childhood. Night was a lovely darkness
cops could never touch—even as they
knocked us over barricades we sang
as if we were being struck by light.

Meachem Road

Body I have refused to look
at you. Since you were nine
and sharp as a splinter. The sky
instead. Falling. A cow on the slope

not weighing anything. Her spine
an ivory flute under all that steak
and leather. I tug on her ear tag
like a father yanking his boy

from the candy rack. My father
before he pretended to get sober.
I wonder. When a cow lies down
is it really going to rain?

Four Lanes

Blue sky. The blue devil in my veins turned red when he reached the heart. As always, I was burning north to meet you. That drive over flattest Illinois felt like navigating Niagara in a broken barrel. All the swimming lessons in the world wouldn't save me. I rattled along, smoking, half-dead, pedal to the floor. Fancy cars flew by like angry swallows, wretched children banging the windows.

Southbound. Behind me the slick spires of the city rose like rockets— shining, deadly, choked with smog. Cornstalks walked the road like Russian refugees. I swore if the radio played that song again I'd rip it out. The listing barns lost their money to the sky, the tire-black clouds fanned out a club flush. Fenced field edges like well-worn decks. I had this pair of eyes, three fingers on the wheel.

The car pulled east like a toy on the assembly line, as trees swung their giant robotic arms above. A woman in the next lane ate her cell phone like one might eat a peach. For thirty seconds I was crushed with love, then a semi came between us and a blast of soulless air grayed the sky from the grooves of my tires to the white underbelly of heaven. All my glossy lovers disappear like that.

I have driven every way but west, the way they always say to go. Insects spatter the windshield, splayed in their armor like dead Greeks, then jets of wiper fluid blast away their epic. I turn the music up so high the speakers buzz and shake the windows, but no bass line can kill the record spinning backward in my head. The gods are flying fast above me, and I'm wishing we had never met.

Woods Beyond the Pond

come upon that white oak
again those graying

rungs we hammered
in the bark

looking for the world
like fossils

and faces rush
back and orange

birds drifting
like ash

in a purple sky
cloud-edges

tinted fire-
bright the rooster's

crown a bloody
saw in the first

branches
a curled fetus

almost born
cut out

or torn
from the murdered

mother
by some animal

we never knew
we never told

Four Names

My name's a scar, an indication, a beacon for travelers and a con man's match. The *x* Blind Lemon used to sign his army papers, the stone he lies forever under. The comment on the lesson and the grade, the place the race begins and the legacy of runners. A monument, a promise, a stoppage in time. It kills the postage, says farewell. It's patsy, gull and German bill—hit it and you win.

Of all Hileni they thought themselves best—*Heleni-wek,* Illiniwek, Illinois. Trudged through head-high grass, raiding and retreating, shouting at the kids, *Stay close,* but still their names fell on the ground—*Peoria, Kaskaskia, Cahokia*—it welcomed them as it will welcome all of us one day. Gave way to *Buckeyes, Hoosiers, Suckers,* stepping like old soldiers in footprints of the dead.

Your name, being youthful, went up the hill with Jack and fell all to the ground with him, you doxy! Think of grinding grain or mother's helper, of dollars, murder and window frames for rhymes. I'm ill when you're away or put your hard face on or fawn on famous men. Your *l*'s are the bars on my fanciful jail cell, my shell, my shill, achilles heel. Your name is excellent, easiest of all to spell.

This vale, this mother dragging children through the store, eyes cracked like spoiled clams, hair piled on her head, spine like a hanging whip. This soil, this word we spin on, clutched kernel burning under a greasy sun. This loam, clunch, muck we shape against night and wind, clay some guru pulled into ilium, ischium, tibia and tarsus. This garbage heap. This miracle. This aching animal.

Eighteen Hours

Bound to a chair I quivered
like the feathers on a wobbly

arrow but stuck
to my story

as a President
will hold a losing war

in his arms like a horrible,
red-faced child

and love it. You said
I was shaking—

nothing would convince
you otherwise, but it was

the nation like a cornered
lunatic shaking all of us.

Night Deaths

Constellations press
into our black curtain.
The city elevators
rocket skyward. Under

a quartz-gemmed ceiling the devil
sits at a metal table, fidgeting
and glum—like a boy forced to man
his sister's lemonade stand.

Shafts empty into pools
of dark around him. People
will always be thirsty.
Patience wins in the end.

Four Wheels

Come on dollar! Come on luck which also gives men cardboard shirts and rat-gray whiskers. I went on worse than Finn but chanced into the palace, pale as a Spanish prince. Come on game show hair! Keep me out of cells, food lines, spats that spill out on police-bright grass. Come on gods. Lay down shingles, thick mattresses, a dog, some leaping children. Leave me be and let the next guy spin.

Imagine rolling room-sized stones on logs for twenty years, watching your friends beaten, crushed, dying from thirst. The curses you'd lash at gods and kings! In the Tombs of Ur a warrior lies beside the bones of his mules and driver. Under cathedral spires which pierce the clouds and mock the whitty pears below, thin King John lies still as an ox horn under a beard of scutage marble.

Heard tell we're crashing one through muddy space, not outer either—from what's in us you can engineer a star. Not that I recommend it. Then you have to watch her die, like every other fucking thing. Or at least wait a million years for her to visit. Better to make small copies of your own flawed self. And about this awful whirling—get used to it. Our carny threw the lever and dropped dead.

I was a thirsty child, but never wanted milk. I never. Does that make me a turtle? They have kids too but don't eat ivy or bleat nocturnes from the hills. No high heaven after all, no winged women sniffing our stink. I am a naughty child, an old school sinner. Dharma, Umma, Bhava, which way the grassy hills? I am a foolish child, trusting fish forever, trusting the voice inside my lover's skin.

Twenty-First Century Vacation

I rake goose shit from the beach
before we settle by the lake.
My mind goes gentle.

Above cobalt water an animated
heron freezes in the sky. Over
the rise, saplings of a tree farm

look like lost dollars
flipping in the breeze.
This year the marvelous

swimwear tramping across
the sparkle in white ear wires
is young enough to be my daughter.

One View

I lurch from bed
in the near
dark. God

these winter
mornings when day
waits at the door

like two
bored officers
while I put on

whatever
clothes are lying
on the floor.

Four Suns

This one fights dirty, burning black the giant elm. We all should lose our leaves and feel light on our gray bones, shed our bomb vests like the man crossing Jackson on arthritic sticks. A Buick skids up to the crosswalk and spooks a crow picking at french fries frozen to the Wendy's parking lot. This one has ideas. She's always trying to improve me. She's only pretty when she glares.

Crayon yellow, skewered with orbits, it hangs above a boy who yells out numbers like a trader at the stock exchange. The scale's completely off, of course. Uranus really should be outside hanging from the swings, thinks the boy, and dreams of Voyager 2—twenty years from Neptune, three hundred thousand from its first star. The teacher calls his name. Pluto's nowhere to be seen.

Red fire we rode toward, under which we sweated out our equatorial adventures. Shrill sound I shied from with my lover—we hadn't even slept! I have watched this sick machine suck shoots through topsoil like missiles from their silos. Many times she's slid down her parents' roof to meet me. Many times I've let her whisper hotly in my ear. She is dying to eat us. She is oiling our skins.

Reverend, leave me be. Go hassle chalk boys puzzling ciphers. My yen for her heels in my back is stronger than your yen to save me. Anyway I thought we came to an agreement— you'd stay out of rooms with proper blinds. You take clapboard houses, bloated rivers, every wet dollar in the mint. I'm not giving up wet tongues. Go preach in a Dictaphone. I'll listen when I'm almost dead.

A Port in Air

Dying fireflies
light the bottom of a jar—

heartless little
bags of blood.

A children's game.
A lantern. When the

medivac chopper
leaps from the hospital

my daughter hears
our prisoners roaring.

After the Attack

The rest of us were rubble or ash.
I wandered paint-chip hieroglyphics
and fortunes of knocked-out glass.
Shoulder over foot, shoulder over foot.

Black choppers lowered their bodies
on the ragged skyline, wind in their wild
hair, then fog blew in like steam
from a cracked pastry.

From behind its curtain: ghost birds
flashing police light from their wingtips,
bloodied girl, and gray tank like a dirty
iceberg bobbing toward the village.

Four Dreams

You should dream more, Mr. Wormold. Reality in our century is not something to be faced.
—Graham Greene

A black mare broke through the forest wall behind my uncle's house, where a creek cut the earth like a brown wound. I used to go down there with my sister and watch her catch bright minnows in her quick fingers. We made a dam of sticks and she got a handful then, where they shimmied like dusk on the house's red shingles, then tumbled down the bank, the big horse splashing after them.

My inner child gets out, starts mucking in the yard with a speculum, working up a mud and wrapper castle between those wild hedges where I buried a baby rabbit then tried to dig it up for bones. When skyscrapers start shooting up around me, I don't need Freud to know I better come to before the shit gets freaky. Heavens, wild trees! Oh where is that naughty mouse who wakes me up?

I undo my skin and hang it on a stick behind the barn where Harold Williams counts out sweaty bills for picking in the orchard, his cigarette poking from his beard like a broken beak. The sky empties its guts on us and we hunker inside with a few dogs and draw from Harold's flask as night blacks out the chink in the wall. I tap my fingers on the shiny surface of my liver, my second heart.

It was a big relief when the world burst into flame. We were cold and soggy, glad of anything that warmed us. Missiles and Mormons, jacket bombers and pervert priests spun on Noah's carousel, maybe the light fantastic. We held our hands to blazing curtains until an old giant shook his hair and blew them out. He had bigger fish to bear. Overturned his water bucket on our heads. I swear.

33

Song

I toss and sweat and thrash away the sheets
under the blade of a bright half-moon,
caught between waking—poplar branches
against yellow siding—and dream,
where a weather-beaten dock shivers in the surge,
whipping dead boats with their own moorings.
Man, this headache's getting good.
You used to run a finger through the gauzy dust
behind the desk and yes, a year of moths
still crumbles on the sills. Now you're off
on your big adventure, your hands on sailors' zippers,
God knows where your mouth. I shine a flashlight
through the house, smashing windowpanes.
The curtains hang like empty sails.

Poem for the Sufferer

Three trees in, a big drift slows you down for good.
Please don't look at the sky.

You do, as if some giant crane will lower
its padded hook and pull you out, or better,

swoop down on space-age wings
and drop a yellowed map.

Heaven's sick blue
presses down like a two-week-old

grown up suddenly in your arms.
Just like I said it would.

Four Accidents

First the car that cracked her back and made the scar my finger found on her right breast. She lay like the hawk of my dreams, wings spanning the ditch while the driver knelt over her, slicing his knees on window glass. Bean plants whispered to black clouds. A breeze rose from the road and turned corn leaves over in the sun, a breath. Across Red Creek, three crows spat out her name.

Your fiance's beltless body leaned to fill the van with a laugh. Shit, a stop sign. Another impact, another bootless cry in a city of accident, where metal and glass run like mercury beside the highway. Your tall tent stake of a man, bent and useless, thrown into the woods to puzzle bears. Crickets, leaf-roar, boots of paramedics. The murmur of a tuning orchestra before the symphony begins.

You won't find them even in the deep pages of the newspaper. A woman slips in the garage with her car running, is ruined like a hail-spoiled apple. A boy flies off his bike in the gravel left by melting snow and leaves his body in the ditch of childhood. A painter falls into a rosebush, never to raise another ladder. A music teacher takes one last methadone, never to bow her violin again.

We're waiting for an invisible galaxy to eat the Milky Way and all its boiling angels, are driven by a god with a golden whip, by jingles and tanned heroes, and punk songs like garbage cans run over by the truck. Let us pray. Let us climb the hill and survey the overpass as Balboa looked upon his ocean, and hearken to the leaves falling like loaded brushes on our ruined promised land.

Poem Ending with a Dilapidated Fence

Light shines through the neighbor's elm
from a sun like a white blister.

The early birds still turn their rusted gears.
Can't they sing something else?

Some mornings all the angles seem correct.
A year ago, power lines lacing from the eaves

wrapped the neighborhood like a gift—
a slight eastern bend to the leaves.

This isn't one of those days. Whatever agonies
I've gone through with others are nothing against

the sun's injury, the creaky song, the dew
like the sweat of a firewalker on my feet.

At the yard's edge, where the ground softens,
the posts march down toward hell, or core.

Oracle

I believe in a future
when the tuba is what the cool
kids play and sounds not like

the fart of UPS trucks in this
dumb town, not like the loser's
last life moan, but like fog rising

up castle walls would sound
if such things were allowed
to bellow. This world

will fall, its flaming guitars
marched to their graves.
The ditches full of tiny phones.

Four Flights

Others become angels at night, because no one has ever called them angels by day.
—Sigmund Freud

Most days are ordinary days, far from the flying we do in dreams. I pay bills under the calendar's checkerboard, noting a few black days ahead. When a sparrow kamikazes the patio door, I go out with a bag to scoop it up. But every night the moon is sharper. I count stars in the plaster ceiling and wait for black angels to open their mouths, brushing steeples and red maples with their wings.

After the deaths, after months of bitter heat, a blast of air from Canada burns south like a comet until only a hint of its icy core stirs the wilted grass. I marvel at the confidence of horses running down a hill, unsaddled, crazy with dust—their muscled chests, their useless, tossing manes, nostrils opened to the wind to the point of pain. As I watch them gallop I fly again, a dead bird in my hand.

Because you are in Tokyo tonight, my charcoal shadow blows smoke across the siding. In your other city, you skip easily from subway to sidewalk, then into the market to escape a morning shower. I stay here, a boy putting pennies on the tracks, waiting. The real train blares and brings me back inside, where you are sleeping after all, eyes alive with some red dream. The house fills up with air.

This time, in May, the concussion of a southbound train cuts off our discussion. You were trying to announce? Nothing now but embers of a forest blaze. The firefighters left. We ran all the matinees of your slight hands. Now we count the clock in tree-time. Off to the annex then, off to the possibility of panic, to experiments with different horsepowers, to *mine* and *his* and *hers* but never ours.

A Simple Mirror

The newspaper scans
my eyes from right to left
like an Iranian
reading about the death

of the last Shah, Pahlavi,
whose message Armstrong
and Aldrin carried
to the moon.

One more first
on the list.
A newspaper
tossing me aside.

My Other Friend

/ thought nothing
of running on the beach
in hurricanes / would require
a cane of course

in age / left me dizzy
as a geometrist
I hated /
who never

did one thing
straight / was always
just one drink
from falling over

Four Deaths

You've heard the womb is warm, but only from escapees who left it behind like a car driven three hundred miles in the heat, the engine ticking madly under its scalding hood. Warm compared to air and earth perhaps. But held up to the hot before and after, the water cools, just as the engine cools there in the desert in the silly dark. After the sun flies off to burn the brittle forests to the west.

The possum was flattened by days of traffic, turning the color of the road. She was out of proportion like a child's drawing, with a tiny mouth and a giant ear. Her one eye shot back a bit of sun as I walked by, holding my breath against the stink. I moved on, against traffic. Cars swung over the yellow line, avoiding me, as the possum stared up into the leaves with her widening stare.

The agents sped like termites in slick black shoes, and sprayed an X on each closed door. I thought the place would go off in one big boom, scattering us into pieces of sun, but they burned us one face at a time, one restaurant, one hovel. The woman on the corner had perfect toenails and spoke to me in ringtones and Navaho ciphers. I denied her proper burial. I fled the killing floor.

When the leaves are the yellow of your feet, kneel in a clearing and cover the back of your neck like you did for the Soviet attack. Be a small brown wart on the skin of the earth. It will be too late for prayers. Only begging then, that the scalded grass may hide you from the horror of bare trees, from the drone-like hawks who circle the dead earth, waiting for some small thing to move them.

Notes from a Tuesday Traffic Jam

I am lost in thin beer, playgrounds of rusting UFOs, gigantic french fry bill-boards, lost in the mall, the wild gyrations of the clock, lost like a stroller out-side 7-11, lost for good in walls of televisions, in slaughtered animals spitting on the grill, in the drugstore's red cursive, the static surf of my computer, lost in bourbon fumes and smog belched from the assholes of Toyotas, in scrolls of city names on airport monitors, in the blips and squiggles of hospital machinery, lost in Sanskrit written on cloud edges,

deep in the slows and downrushes of my mind, in forests northern and tropical, topical and forgotten, in the slender past, where dogs and sofas and crushes and jeans and parents and bones and nations are all young,

banned from the thoughts of old lovers who smuggle through cities their pills for headaches, brainfevers, liveraches, heartaches, birth control, better orgasms, stomach trouble, sleeplessness and panic attacks, who carry neon cell phones, pagers, stethoscopes, bible verses, nail clippers, pepper spray, scrawled phone numbers, airline vodka and Virginia Woolf, recipes for Mai Tais and chicken korma and fancified mashed potatoes, photographs of dogs, lovers, husbands, girlfriends, fathers and mothers, of men in hats and foreign-looking women, of cats, roller coasters, antique toasters, sailboats, cruise ships, Sarasota beaches and African airports, but not one photo, even crumpled and by accident, of me,

abandoned by the dead who gamble every night, who eat what they want, who burn their trash for extra light, who write hundred-act plays then dump them for a game of tennis, who pump the scent of perfume, corn bread, pipe smoke, azal-eas, old clothes, salt air, moth balls, trampled violets, factory wind, deodorant, gunpowder, and my own dying skin into the air, left behind by Paris Hilton and Sherman tanks, Volkswagens and Kremlin and Martyr's Mosque, by the hormone-pumped thighs of Sammy Sosa and Tyson chicken, by the sharp edge on my neighbor's lawn, by the blather of cell phones zinging the air, the TV talk, the breasts and plastic and dismembered corpses and Hollywood limos and flattened earthquake villages and shiny dogs and bleeding diamonds all zinging the air like fairies, by the President's coded messages zinging around the world, believers zinging him back with puckish missiles, all of them zinging away my beloved ghosts who move through air awkward and slow and are no match,

rotting like a banana in a high school locker, like a minefield in a mountain pass, like open wine, like ideology, like the bones of an extinct woodpecker, like a deer lost in a field of thistles, like old tires, like the stooped woman there with her little dog, her rotting little dog,

sung by the last stray cat in her heat, by an old soprano to an empty room, by wintering crickets, by soaked maple leaves, by kids fleeing the school bus into the dying sun, sung by the murmuring drunk in the back row of the movie theater, by the band at a high school prom, sung softly by the last tired wedding guest, his tie drooping from his hand;

I am hidden in the face of the moon.

Four Mothers

Canny pigs dug up the garden, bristling, eyes sunk in their muddy mugs. Foreign ladybugs squeezed through loose siding, dug in through the crawlspace for all I know, turned warm and drunk on our windowsills. Our red maple—so goddamn handsome—wouldn't look me in the eye. Its leaves shook in the wind like riotous prisoners. A week later they were gone. Just like your father.

I was running late, left the boy to piss the beanbag chair and suffered the looks of daycare girls, made-up bitches with skin like new car doors. He popped the Alice pill that grows you ten years in a flash. During the funny song I cried, when Alice wept a lake I laughed. After I stroked his hair to sleep, I sat in front of the computer and saw the reflection of new wrinkles around my eyes.

I'm at the bedside, graveside of the baby never born, whispering prayers that fly up through the canopy like red balloons or burrow in the soft soil of the family plot like those moles who keep digging Uncle up. Broadside of grief I fire shells that leave impossible black suns on its massive iron plating. I'm mountainside, fireside, subsiding like a summer storm. I'm homicide, wailing at the prison door.

One open eye. The breath of children fills the house like paper factories fill a town with stink, like ice storms turn grass to glass. I dreamed I ran a marathon up a tree fallen through the roof. The dead ran too, in fine shape, flying by like highway cars. What does that mean? Outside the garbage truck banged along, downstairs the heavy drawer opened—things I would banish if I were queen.

45

The World Without Me

Feels a little better. The robin
I ran over this morning
returns to its poplar nest.
There's one extra seat on the bus,
one more job, another available lover.
Less spit and shit.

The planet still trudges around the sun.
My mother has more money,
R. J. Reynolds, less.

Areas of grass remain unworn.
All my thoughts—sluggish
and sublime—can rest,
unborn. The sidewalk
(where my shadow fell)
shines.

I Pass You on the Street

Under my white shirt
—bright as a policeman's
flashlight—is a grumbling,
skittish dog, the kind you see

sulking in alleys,
bristling if you near
its dumpster. You think
me a pity

and hurry past,
sticking close to the wall,
because you also know
enough to be afraid.

Four Threads

*We hold several threads in our hands, and the odds are that one
or other of them guides us to the truth.*
   —Sherlock Holmes

My fingers shook as I tied thread around a giant hinge. Its unraveling tickled my thumb like fishing line while my other hand bumped along the wall. Outside a sun-blind driver nearly crushed the fire-haired woman and her son. She huddled to the wall and held the boy below my window, waiting for the fuming king. Woman caught my eye like a spinner wakes a bass, left me airless, reeling.

Hounds are hard to recall once they catch a scent. The dog scuffs up a path and I remember walking toward faint music at a fair, knowing it was her favorite music, knowing she was there. On stage the drummer's sweat flew like swarming insects in the lights. She watched his hands, her eyes as big as hornet nests. I hid behind a tree. How terrible to catch the thing you're after.

Watson says if life gives you lemons make vodka tonics, and through the long wire I crackle, *Come here, I want to see you.* It's good to have a sidekick, slapstick, a good Friday to break the coconuts. Dearest Thomas, you fill me with liquor-soaked fruit, then want me to solve it, to get my voice across the canyon. But this hum is a howling—black and garbled, lit with phosphorus.

Exiting the maze was a wild hurry. Afterwards I felt relief, but no elation. I followed a line, that's all. And the beast was hobbled, his great warty feet no match for my new-fangled shoes. Back on board we opened a keg of beer. The fire-haired woman sat with her jeweled fingers on my leg. But she was already sneaking looks at the horizon. I had no thread left to follow but the wind.

Beneath the City

In the subway tunnel
rudderless cars
thudded above my head
like dreams.

I made a promise
to the rats. I said
the food was awful
up there. People

ducked the sun
like rebel
flowers, too
strung out to care.

Kankakee

Real boys lurked
in Pontiacs and spat

about the jacked-up
smoke tax, smacked

packs in their palms,
lit crooked sticks

they stole
from 7-11 jobs

with just one match
like we scouts

were rumored to light
our campfires.

Four Moons

When the sun blew silver from the roofs of riverside lowrises, I slipped into a Baptist church. Penitents moved to a rough hymn their royal lips. Bats poured from the ruined eaves at dusk, dark angels spreading out to heal the Southside sick, to lay the sleepless in their beds. Sundays they dozed above the pipes as the organ sputtered and droned clear to the river, sluggish and brown.

In studio the actors mill while camera roughs trail miles of baled black wire. Behind a pane the bosses bully phones, crush paper cups in wrinkled fingers. This cannot be the right appointment. The star shoots in, shorter than I thought but stunning, like a smooth green tree in the middle of a desert. From a distance he looks hollow but I worm in close enough to touch—he's heavier than lead.

Bedrooms and hay barns, basement couches and backseats of cars that cough and spit up Avery Hill. Insurance company meeting rooms. Awful attics. The light always yellow, a taste on the tongue like foil. If there is a roof (not so in meadows, glades) and rain, it turns into a timpani, a glorious attack. If there is sun it burns like spitting oil. On cloudy days, cymbals crashing overhead.

Near four hundred pounds upon this dust and light as an Ohio sparrow. So glad you touched down too. Being first isn't everything, ain't anything at all. Being is the thing, brother. Never shall we tell (we'll hide it in our graying hair), but there were creatures there, slight as starving children— our piano footprints took up four of theirs. They had no use for giant leaps. They were everywhere.

Strange Craft

My crib was cosmos.

I wrestled its cruel laws
with squat red hands.

You think it was dismantled?

Packed up and stashed
in the attic or carted off

in the back of a truck?

Cut into my skin, then
break the breastplate

to find the cage around
the place where others

store their hearts.

Chamber

When you talk like that
you remind me of the shotgun
I used to shoot
your new boyfriend.

It was an accident!
If you've read this before, I'm sorry.
No one can predict a ricochet
or next week's

movie times. We should
catch a flick. You're so
serious, so hollow.
I put a flower in your barrel.

Four Horses

The first bears a warrior across salt flats, at the behest of the senator, the manager pulling up his pants. Columbia's a bright bird ahead, slamming face-first into the atmosphere. With metal and bone fragments float down roundworms and moss. He believes in robes and whales, in waves smashing rock as natives spy on spectral foreheads rowing into shore, noses breathing over beard-brown holes.

The jobless man sketches a horse on his boy's wall, fills it in with the red of cave paintings. Once he thought he'd be an artist. Or a soldier. Uncle Renny in his sweaty trailer cured him quick of that. Told about a bullet he put in the forehead of a grandmother, how that hole kept pouring red in his dreams. The man wipes his hand on his shirt, gets a beer, watches wildfires burn the TV screen.

Electric bulbs throw quavering eggs of light on the pine floors, and out come coyotes, owls, windowless vans and swat rams bashing doors. The black horse carries a cop of course, his radio breaking up the sleeping park where he comes upon the Mexican kid, calls backup, buddies he'll drink Buds with after. Time to close shutters, turn up the game. You don't want a part in this.

A wild dusty horse—flesh, scream—rips a hole in the blue, and a gang of gray-robed women follow. I clench the silver of the operating table—a pill I shouldn't have taken. Tear away the plastic mask and there's the doctor, ventilator dangling at her side. Into her eyes we go, riding hard over plains where clouds billow from the horizon like factory smoke. Ahead the green swath bordering a river.

Memory

Not the light of heaven
but a definite glow
before I fall asleep—
the mind's Milky Way,

fading in the daylight
of a dream. My friend died.
I put a dollar in the casket,
then went to one knee like a squire.

The path around the church
burned its electric coil
in the unblocked sun
and I forgot his name.

The Book of Paradise

What a drag—
exiled to heaven
while my lover
cascades down

the long duct
skimming her
fingers on its
metal sides,

ringing them
like a crystal glass.
I have eaten fifty thousand
tulips waiting.

Four Furies

No god there is to teach such herd as you.
—Aeschylus

Out from the poles these furies fly and boil the ice into oceans. Meanwhile I'm buying shoes, my feet propped on the inclined stool like a ragged king's, the moans of mountains under them. Our migratory birds just fly in circles now, from parks to dumpsters to rooftop pools. At night I take off and drive the cornfields outside town, as passing refugees form a little range above the road.

The elders rough me up and drag me through woods as dark as buried bones. My genes feel like a bag of diamonds left in the will of a crotchety grandfather as I'm marched to a clearing where husbands rooster dance, wine leaking from their mouths. You tip over in the fire, then screech at me like an arrow, breasts burning, eyes melting like arctic ice, a flaming finger pointed at my chest.

We turn off the light and fight in the dark about the same old nothing, turning the nasty splinters we planted at the break of winter. I'm crass, like my friend whose wife had a two-year affair with the bedroom wall. He thought every woman was a pornstar or a prude. You say I have no friends and roll away as this week's angels cackle outside our window, shapeshifting to shooting stars.

The woman I love is impossible with these three flying low above my head, with the oceans steaming in the ovens of the coast. I love them more, and realize I'm like every hero now—the wishes that come true undo me. I feel their heat on my broken face. The furies giggle and scrap like girls at the back of a bus. *Child, child, child* they chant, as we drive through fields of violent light.

Acknowledgments

Thank you to the editors of the following journals, where some of these poems first appeared, sometimes in different forms:

Birmingham Poetry Review: "Four Lanes"
Boulevard: "Four Furies"
Cimarron Review: "Lovers' Meal" and "Funeral"
Columbia Poetry Review: "Four Blues"
DoubleTake: "Four Dreams" and "Four Mirrors"
FIELD: "Four Falls"
Great River Review: "Poem Ending with a Dilapidated Fence"
Hunger Mountain: "Notes from a Tuesday Traffic Jam"
Indiana Review: "Four Accidents"
Meridian: "Four Threads"
Natural Bridge: "Four Flights"
New Orleans Review: "Four Years" and "Song"
Perigee: "Cardinal"
The Pinch: "I Pick a Fist-Fight with the Sky"
Poets and Artists: "Einstein's Alphabet," "One View," and "The Book of Paradise"
River Oak Review: "The World Without Me"
Salt Hill: "Memory"
Southeast Review: "Four Fields"
Texas Poetry Journal: "After the Attack"
West Branch: "Four Deaths"

Some of these poems also appeared in a chapbook, *Four of a Kind,* published by Concrete Wolf Press in 2010.

I am grateful to David Walker and David Young for their belief in my work, to my teachers, especially Bruce Smith and Robin Behn, for their generous guidance, and to Tim Earley for his friendship and sage advice. To Mom, Dad, Sophia, Juliet, Martha Christman, Pete Christman, and Sean Lovelace for their love and support. And to Jill, Ella, and Henry for every day.